INNOVATORS

Chad Hurley, Steve Chen, Jawed Karim

YouTube Creators

Other titles in the Innovators series include:

Seamus Blackley and J. Allard: Xbox Developers
Tim Burton: Filmmaker
Jonathan Ive: Designer of the iPod
Ken Kutaragi: PlayStation Developer
Stephanie Kwolek: Creator of Kevlar
John Lasseter: Pixar Animator
Shigeru Miyamoto: Nintendo Game Designer
Pierre M. Omidyar: Creator of eBay
Larry Page and Sergey Brin: The Google Guys
Burt Rutan: Aircraft Designer
Shel Silverstein: Poet
Frederick W. Smith: Founder of FedEx
Satoshi Tajiri: Pokémon Creator
Osamu Tezuka: God of Manga Comics

INNOVATORS

Chad Hurley, Steve Chen, Jawed Karim

YouTube Creators

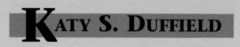

Katy S. Duffield

KIDHAVEN PRESS
A part of Gale, Cengage Learning

GALE
CENGAGE Learning™

Detroit • New York • San Francisco • New Haven, Conn • Waterville, Maine • London

GALE
CENGAGE Learning

LIBRARY OF CONGRESS CATALOGING-IN-PUBLICATION DATA

Duffield, Katy S.
Chad Hurley, Steve Chen, Jawed Karim : YouTube creators / by Katy S. Duffield.
p. cm. — (Innovators)
Includes bibliographical references and index.
ISBN 978-0-7377-4270-1 (hardcover)
1. Hurley, Chad, 1977– 2. Chen, Steve, 1978– 3. Karim, Jawed, 1979– 4. Telecommunications engineers—United States—Biography—Juvenile literature. 5. Webmasters—United States—Biography—Juvenile literature. 6. Computer programmers—United States—Biography—Juvenile literature. 7. Businesspeople—United States—Biography—Juvenile literature. 8. YouTube (Electronic resource)—Juvenile literature. 9. YouTube (Firm)—Juvenile literature. 10. Internet videos—Juvenile literature. 11. Online social networks—Juvenile literature. I. Title.
TK5102.54.D84 2009
384.3'3—dc22
[B]

2008029079

KidHaven Press
27500 Drake Rd.
Farmington Hills, MI 48331

ISBN-13: 978-0-7377-4270-1
ISBN-10: 0-7377-4270-4

Printed in the United States of America
2 3 4 5 6 7 12 11 10 09

Contents

Introduction

A Video Sharing Phenomenon

Coworkers Steve Chen, Chad Hurley, and Jawed Karim probably never thought they would be in the position they are in right now. When they were in their twenties, the three men came up with a unique idea and worked long hours to develop a product that would change the way the world viewed and shared videos. They called their creation YouTube.

The YouTube service provides users with a fast, simple way to **upload** and share videos they have created. Once a user has uploaded content, the videos are available for the world to see. A quick visit to the Web site reveals that a wide variety of video content can be found on the site: political speeches, sports, music videos, travel clips, current events such as clips from the Iraq war, comedy, crazy animal antics, and much more.

According to Chen, Hurley, and Karim, they developed the site in hopes that YouTube would "entertain, inform and empower the world through video."[1] And this is just what they did. When YouTube was first launched in 2005, viewers watched an

Steve Chen, left, Chad Hurley, right, and Jawed Karim (not pictured) created YouTube, a service that allows users to upload and share videos.

estimated 10 million videos a day. Two years later that number rose to over 100 million videos viewed every single day. As to what the men attribute this amazing success, Chen says it is simple: "Everybody wants to be a star."[2]

Chapter 1

The YouTube Story

Creative thinking and a lot of hard work led Steve Chen, Chad Hurley, and Jawed Karim to develop the service now known as YouTube. From its beginnings, with the three young men working in Hurley's garage, to its current far-reaching success, these three came together as coworkers and friends, developed an idea, and did not stop until they reached their goals.

The Early Days

Chen, Hurley, and Karim first met and became friends in 2004 while working at an online payment service called PayPal. On one particular evening, Chen and Hurley attended a dinner party in San Francisco. While at the party, the men shot some video of the party guests. The next day Chen and Hurley tried to find an easy way to share the video with friends, but they ran into problems. The files were too large to be sent through e-mail. And even if they could have been sent, their friends might have had trouble opening the files because of the differing formats of media players.

These problems led to an interesting idea. Hurley and Chen thought if they had trouble sending videos, other people might have the same problem. They knew online video sharing was not a completely new idea, but for the most part, there was no easy way to go about it. According to Chen, "The pieces to make it all happen just weren't in place until we came around."[3] Hurley added that if they wanted the new service to be successful, the upload process would have to "be a no-brainer."[4]

With the idea fresh in their minds, Chen and Hurley, along with Jawed Karim, set out to find a solution. The men first worked out details and strategies in Hurley's garage. After a period of time, they came up with a way to take videos in any format and play them on just about any computer. The YouTube site uses something called flash technology, a program that is already installed on most computers. The decision to use this particular technology ensured that almost anyone could access the video content placed on the site.

An Overnight Success

At first, Chen, Hurley, and Karim thought their service might be of use to people who wanted to sell items on the Internet. Videos could be taken of a product and then uploaded to an online auction site where buyers could bid on the item. The men knew they had a promising product, but at that point, they did not have any idea where their creation would lead them. Each man played a unique role in the development process. Hurley came up with the YouTube name and **logo**, while Chen and Karim shared technical duties for the project.

In late 2005, when the partners felt everything was in place, the very first video was uploaded to the YouTube Web site. That simple, eighteen-second video contained a clip of Jawed Karim standing in front of an elephant pen at a California zoo. Hurley later laughed about that first video and said, "Lucky for us, we didn't leave it up to our videos to build the popularity of the site. We allowed our users to contribute videos [instead]."[5]

In December 2005 the partners officially launched the YouTube Web site. After only a few months, more and more people began uploading videos to the site, and YouTube quickly became a household name. At first the men were surprised by the site's popularity. Chen said he thought the video sharing would be on a smaller scale, such as parents uploading videos of their children for their distant relatives to view. He said the concept of "sharing with the world"[6] took them by surprise. One of the reasons the site became **viral**, or spread so rapidly,

The YouTube Web site was launched in December 2005 and was an instant success.

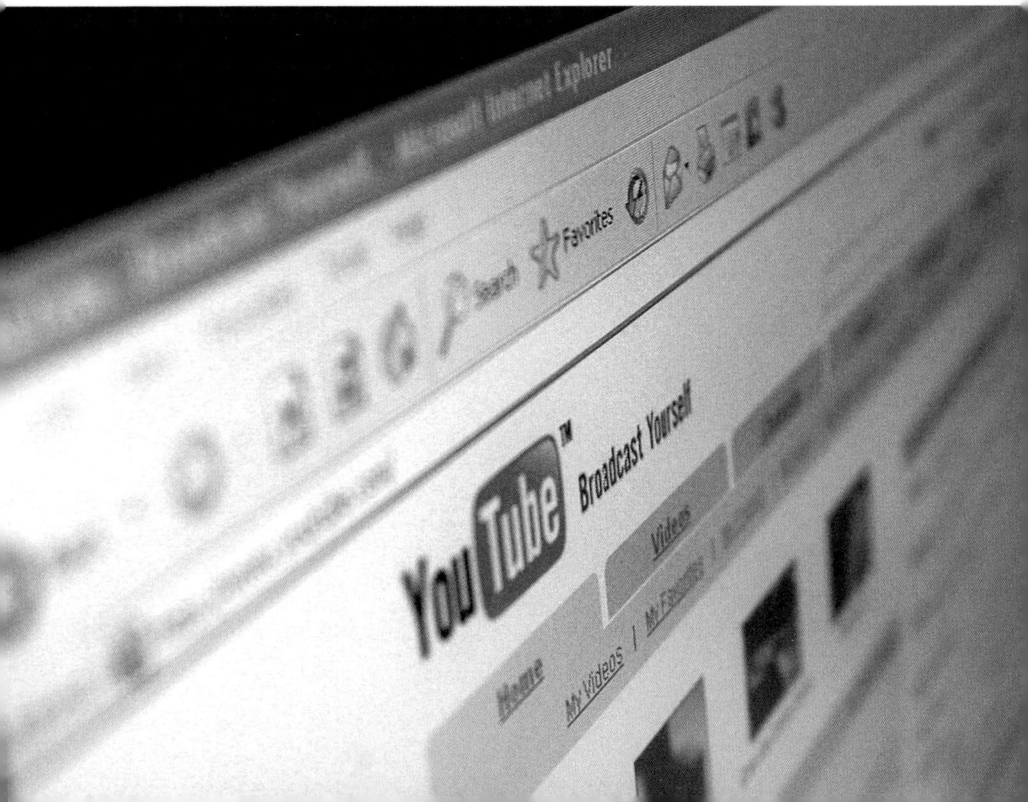

was because users could easily embed, or attach, their videos to other sites such as their **blogs**, personal Web sites, and MySpace pages.

Other reasons for the rapid success of the site came from the fact that there are no user costs and nothing to download, and the site is easy to use. Another bonus is that the site is **interactive**. Viewers are able to rate and comment on any videos they watch. Hurley says, "It's the viewers who decide what is entertaining to them."[7]

Trials and Triumphs

As the YouTube site continued to grow, Chen, Hurley, and Karim grew along with it. Hurley was named chief executive officer (CEO) of the company, and Chen took the position of chief technology officer (CTO). Even though the site was an obvious

Due to the rapid growth of YouTube, several problems arose for the Web site. Copyright infringement, specifically users uploading clips of television shows and films that did not belong to them, was a big problem for the Web site.

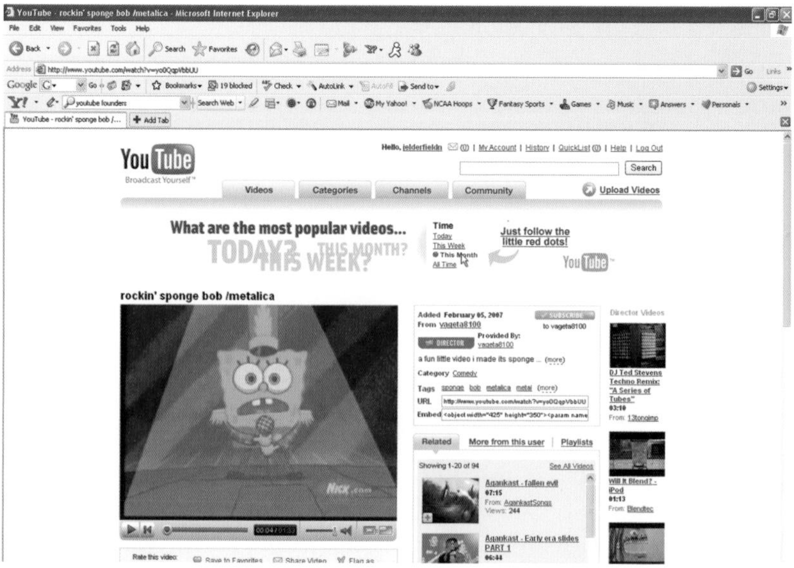

achievement for the partners, Karim had other ideas about his future. Instead of choosing to become part of the YouTube management team, Karim stepped down in order to further his education. Even without Karim, the business thrived. The company's first office was located above a pizza restaurant. In its early days the company employed around 20 people and, according to some reports, one rubber chicken. Over time the number of employees increased to nearly 70.

The partners were thrilled with the growth of their new business, but that growth did not come without its share of problems. One of the main issues that troubled the site was that some users uploaded clips that did not belong to them, such as video clips of films or television shows. This use of material without permission, called **copyright infringement**, is against the law. With the huge number of videos being uploaded every day, it was impossible for YouTube employees to monitor every clip that was posted. The only option Chen and Hurley had was to issue a policy stating if an owner found copyrighted material on the site and notified the management at YouTube, the content would be removed. According to Hurley, the employees at YouTube are continually "developing tools and putting process[es] in place to control what's going on in the site. We ban repeat infringers."[8]

Positive Changes

But along with the bad came the good. After a while, instead of fighting over copyright issues, many companies decided to partner with YouTube. The executives of these companies realized that the effect of having their videos seen by hundreds of thousands of people each day was great advertising for their

Many awards have been given to YouTube and its founders, including the 2007 Webby Special Achievement Award.

products. The YouTube site also began promoting social issues such as antidrug messages, cancer prevention, environmental awareness, and an antibullying campaign. It even became a way for citizens to interact with presidential candidates.

Over a two year period, YouTube and its founders were honored with a long list of awards. These included the 2007 Webby Special Achievement Award, the 2006 *Entertainment Weekly*'s Entertainer of the Year, *PC World*'s 50 Most Important People on the Web for 2007, and *Time* magazine's 2006 Invention of the Year and 100 Most Influential People of the Year.

Growth and Change

Due to its incredible growth and success, YouTube and its founders quickly became noticed by bigger, more well-established Internet businesses. One of those businesses was Google, one of the world's largest Internet search engines. Google had developed its own video sharing service, but it had not enjoyed the huge success that YouTube had. In late 2006 Google made a decision that would change the lives of Chen, Hurley, and Karim. Google purchased YouTube for $1.65 billion.

Since Chen, Hurley, and Karim were primary owners in the company, they all earned great profits. Estimates say Hurley and Chen made around $300 million each from the sale. Since Karim owned a smaller share of the company than Hurley and Chen, his profit was not as high, but he revealed that his share was still quite large.

In 2006, Google purchased YouTube for $1.65 billion. Chen and Hurley continued working for YouTube after the sale.

In some cases, when a business is sold, the former owners leave the company and find other work. But in this case, Chen and Hurley continued working for the Google-owned YouTube. According to Chen, since the Google purchase, their work hours have not diminished. Both Chen and Hurley agree they still work as hard, or harder, than they did at the site's start-up.

One of the major projects they have taken on since the Google buyout was the launching of local sites in such areas as Brazil, France, Ireland, Italy, Japan, the Netherlands, Poland, Spain, and the UK. According to Chen, "We're really excited to now offer that same great service to a global community, by bringing them local sites that not only promote their communities but speak their language."[9]

Chapter 2

Steve Chen

When Steve Chen was about six years old, his mother took him to visit a fortune-teller. During their visit, the woman gave Chen some disturbing news. She told him he would never be a rich man. What the fortune-teller did not know was that Chen's drive, intelligence, and reputation as a risk taker would lead him a long way in business and would eventually make him wealthy.

Early Life

Steve Shih Chen was born in Taiwan in 1978. Chen says he remembers very little of his time in Taiwan, because he and his family moved to the United States when he was only eight years old. Chen's father owned a trading business in Taiwan, and when he decided to start up a branch of the company in the United States, the family moved to Chicago. Chen spoke no English when he and his family arrived in the United States, but he had no problem picking up the new language. By the time he was in the third grade, Chen could speak English.

When Chen was in the seventh grade, he made a very important decision. He became a U.S. citizen. His days in Chicago were spent going to school and immersing himself in his new culture. Until he was in junior high, Chen was the only Asian in the schools he attended. Chen mentions in an interview that his life was somewhat different because he lived one culture at school and another one at home. At home, he and his parents spoke Mandarin Chinese, but at school, he spoke English. But, Chen states, even though he was not born in the United States, he never felt "any different from any other kid growing up in the Midwest."[10]

Education and Employment

At thirteen, Chen moved away from home to attend a boarding school called the Illinois Mathematics and Science Academy (IMSA). IMSA was a technologically advanced, highly competitive school. In 1993 it was one of the first schools fully wired for Internet service. According to one source, IMSA is "more like a college than a high school," where students "spend every possible second on the Internet"[11] in order to gain new insights into technology. Each Wednesday, instead of attending regular classes, students at IMSA participated in a self-exploration program so they could focus on and experiment in other areas of study. Chen enjoyed his time at IMSA, but says, "This was the time I learned I wasn't the smartest kid anymore."[12]

As graduation from IMSA approached, Chen applied to only one college—the University of Illinois at Urbana-Champaign. Chen estimates that 60 to 70 percent of IMSA students go on to attend this university, so he never really thought about applying elsewhere. Chen was accepted and enrolled in the university. He began working toward a degree in computer science.

Steve Chen was born in Taiwan, but his family moved to the United States, where young Chen became a United States citizen.

With only one and a half semesters of college left to complete before his graduation, Chen decided to leave school in order to take a job with an Internet payment service called PayPal. Chen's family worried about his decision to leave school early, but Chen was determined to give PayPal a try. Many University of Illinois at Urbana-Champaign graduates worked there, and Chen felt the opportunity was too good to pass up.

Before finishing his college degree, Chen left the University of Illinois at Urbana-Champaign to work for PayPal, an Internet payment service site.

One of PayPal's cofounders, Max Levchin, is the man who hired Chen. He said Chen was someone who could find the "shortest, cleverest path instead of hammering [his] head against the wall."[13] Chen describes his job at the company as a **jack-of-all-trades**. He was an engineer who did whatever it took to make sure the site was kept up and running. One of Chen's biggest projects at PayPal was helping the company launch a PayPal site in China. His other notable accomplishment there was befriending two coworkers—Chad Hurley and Jawed Karim.

YouTube

Chen had worked at PayPal for about seven years when he, Hurley, and Karim came up with the YouTube idea. The men worked tirelessly during their spare time to develop the site. In some ways Chen had more at stake with the YouTube project than his two friends did. Early on in the process, the partners used Chen's credit card to pay for the project's start-up costs. Chen says at some point they were supposed to swap the charges to one of the other men's accounts, but that never happened. For Chen this meant that if something went wrong, he was responsible for repayment. But, fortunately for Chen, everything went smoothly. Start-up costs were expensive, and the credit card debt quickly grew, but the men stuck together. The mounting debt motivated the men to work 80 to 90 hours each week so they could make sure the bills were paid.

As the site was launched and eventually grew, Chen was named chief technology officer (CTO) for the company. Before Karim's departure, he and Chen shared the company's technical duties. When Karim returned to school, Chen took on all the

Hurley (left), Chen (right), and Karim worked on their YouTube idea during their spare time. Once Karim left, Chen took over all technical aspects of the site.

technical aspects of the site. His duties included engineering and managing operations, developing products, and developing new and easy-to-use services for the site. Once the initial development was complete, Chen continued to study new ways to improve the workings of the site.

Life with YouTube

Chen and his partners knew that if the site was going to become a success, they needed to come up with a product that people would use on a daily basis. All three men dedicated themselves to developing strategies to make the product cost effective, making the site easy for consumers to use, and figuring out ways to get people to use the site. They also continued to work on the quality of the site. Higher quality video was the next step in their process. All of this attention to detail has allowed YouTube to become an amazing part of **pop culture**. It certainly

High quality and attention to detail have helped make YouTube a success. The site has the sixth-largest audience on the Internet.

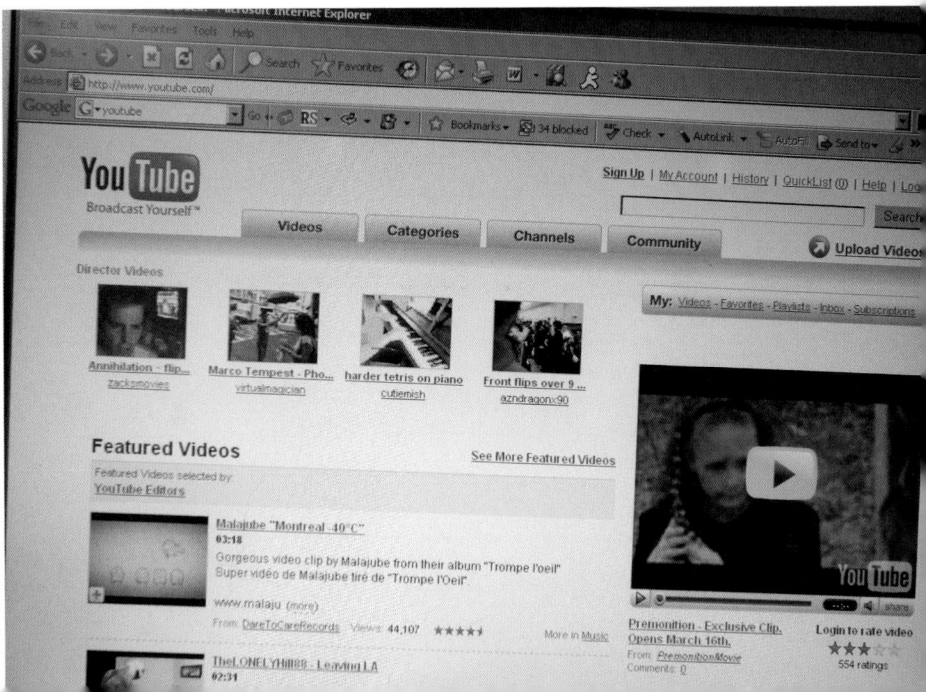

looks as if the men's work has paid off—YouTube has the sixth-largest audience on the Internet, and the average user visits the site between 16 and 33 minutes a day.

When Google bought out YouTube in 2006, it seemed as if major changes were in store for Chen and the others. The buy-out process moved quickly, and Chen barely had time to stop and reflect on what was happening and what it meant for him. Google's purchase of the company has no doubt made Chen a very rich man, but in many ways, his life is just as it was before. Chen and Hurley stayed on with YouTube and continue to work as hard as ever. When Chen looks back, he says it is difficult to believe that only a short time ago, he, Hurley, and Karim were developing the YouTube idea in Hurley's garage.

Chapter 3

Chad Hurley

Chad Hurley is unique in that he possesses both an artsy, creative side and a technical, business side. Chad's mix of imagination and professionalism played an important role during YouTube's start-up and has continued to benefit the site's day-to-day operations.

Early Life

Chad Meredith Hurley was born in 1977 in Birdsboro, a town in southeastern Pennsylvania. Hurley was the middle child of father Donald Hurley and mother JoAnn Hurley. Hurley's father worked as a financial consultant and his mother taught school. Hurley points to his father as his role model. He says his father "encouraged him to try things . . . and taught me the power of positive thinking."[14] These traits helped Hurley believe in himself and gave him the confidence to take chances when pursuing the YouTube development.

As a child, the creative Hurley enjoyed working on different types of art projects. He spent time painting with watercolors

Chad Hurley was a creative child with many different interests, including art, computers, and electronics.

and creating sculptures. At a young age, Hurley made his first attempt at combining his artistic and business talents. Hurley says, "I painted pictures that I tried to sell from my parents' front lawn." When asked if he was successful, Hurley continues, "I don't think I sold any."[15] But this setback did not stop Hurley from pursuing his dreams.

Even though Hurley excelled in creative areas, he had many varied interests. Along with artwork, he enjoyed computers. As a young man, Hurley spent a lot of time surfing the Internet. Although he enjoyed playing computer games, he also had an interest in computer animation and Web design. He liked to study popular Web sites to figure out why designers made the choices they made and which concepts made particular sites and animations successful.

In addition to computers, Hurley also had an interest in electronics. When Hurley was in ninth grade, he built an amplifier that he entered in a national electronics competition. When the winners were announced, Hurley was pleased to discover his amplifier had placed third in the competition.

As if Hurley did not have enough to keep him busy, he also had another passion—running. Hurley competed and excelled in cross-country and track while a student at Twin Valley High School. Hurley graduated from Twin Valley in 1995 and continued running throughout his college years.

Education and Employment

After high school, Hurley attended college at Indiana University of Pennsylvania. Early on, Hurley concentrated on a computer science major, but later switched to graphic design and printmaking. Hurley's father said of the switch, "Computer science, that was too technical, too mechanical for Chad. He wanted to be on the creative side."[16]

In addition to his studies, Hurley continued to excel at sports. He was a member of the cross-country and track and field teams all four years. During college, Hurley's passion for computers continued as well. Hurley spent his spare time exploring how different Web designers developed online sites. He also looked more into the world of computer animation. Hurley studied the sites down to the smallest details in order to discover what made them popular and successful. This study no doubt helped him when development began on the YouTube site.

Along with his studies, Hurley worked for a time while in college. To make some spending money, Hurley got a job selling kitchen knives. Hurley's brother, Brent, jokes that he remembers when Hurley visited his friends' houses to demonstrate the knives. Sometimes Hurley would show the cutting strength of the knives by using them to cut through soda cans. Some of those friends who bought the knives find it interesting that Hurley went from selling knives door-to-door to the CEO of one of the fastest-growing online companies—YouTube.

In 1999 Hurley graduated from college with a bachelor's degree in fine arts. Around the time of his graduation, Hurley heard about a new online payment company called PayPal. He submitted his résumé to the company, and two days later the company flew Hurley to California for an interview. In order to get a better idea of Hurley's artistic talents, the people at PayPal asked him to design and draw up a logo for the company. After viewing the finished product, PayPal's CEO hired Hurley as the company's first designer. The PayPal logo Hurley designed is still in use.

During his interview for PayPal, Hurley designed a logo for the company. As a result, he was hired as the company's first designer. His logo is still in use today.

Since the PayPal job was Hurley's first job out of college, things were not easy the first few weeks. Hurley did not have enough money for apartment rent. He slept on the floor at a friend's place while he awaited his first paycheck. Some sources say he even had to scrounge up money for a pizza dinner. Eventually, however, Hurley's work paid off. As an employee at PayPal, Hurley met his future YouTube partners, Steve Chen and Jawed Karim.

YouTube

During their time at PayPal, Hurley and Chen became good friends. They spent a lot of time together and often discussed ideas for various business **ventures**. When the online auction company, eBay, bought out PayPal, Hurley, Chen, and Karim received large bonuses for their work at the company. Hurley and Chen decided to use some of the money they had received to go into business together. After their legendary dinner party, where the video sharing site idea was born, this money was the backing they needed for the start-up of YouTube.

Hurley came up with the YouTube name and designed its logo.

In the early days of YouTube, Hurley came up with the site name and designed its clean, trendy logo. Hurley got the idea for the site's name when he thought about the slang name for television—"boob tube." Hurley thought that, since the users would be the actual stars of the site, *You*Tube seemed an appropriate name. As the business grew, Hurley was named CEO. As CEO, Hurley was responsible for business development, marketing, and company operations.

Hurley believes that one of the main benefits of the YouTube site is that just about anyone can produce, edit, and share his or her creativity and videos with the world. As a creative person himself, Hurley recognizes the importance of this experience. After the death of a high school friend, Hurley began thinking more about his own life. He says, "Life is short and you can't take anything for granted. . . . [It is] important to live every day to the fullest."[17] And Hurley is doing just that. He says their work at YouTube has only begun, and they want to continue to work to give users the best experience ever.

Chapter 4

Jawed Karim

Jawed Karim is probably the least well known of the YouTube founders. Early on in the site's development, Karim decided to take a different route from the others. Consumed by a passion for computers and learning, Karim recognized the opportunity of YouTube, yet knew he would not be satisfied until he fulfilled his education.

Early Life

Jawed Karim was born in Merseberg, East Germany, in 1979. Shortly thereafter, Karim and his family moved to West Germany, where he spent his childhood. In 1992 the family moved to the United States, where they made their home in St. Paul, Minnesota.

It is easy to see where Karim may have gotten his interest in science. Karim's father, Naimul, is a chemist at the 3M Corporation. His mother, Christine, is a biochemistry research professor at the University of Minnesota. Karim's father says he often took Karim to work with him at his lab. Karim's father mentions that Karim enjoyed playing with various lab items such as a "magnetic stirring bar in a beaker of water."[18] Karim's mother adds that other scientists at the lab always commented on how dedicated he was to learning. She says, "Karim was almost like a sponge. At ten, eleven years old, he would just

Jawed Karim, right, developed an interest in science, computers, and technology at a young age.

listen and observe everything."[19] Even at a young age, Karim's obsession with technology was obvious.

Throughout his school years, Karim's love for science and technology continued. His parents remember that he was constantly working on one science project or another. He also took an interest in computers at a young age. When Karim was ten years old, his father bought him a used computer. After only a short time, Karim began writing his own software code. Karim's interest in computers and technology continued throughout his high school years.

Karim mentions that he has no real secret when it comes to the projects on which he works. He says he mainly concentrates on developing ideas he believes will be useful in his own life, and sometimes other people find those products useful as well.

Education and Employment

Karim attended St. Paul Central High School in Minnesota. When he was sixteen, Karim overheard teachers at his school complaining. They were unhappy because they did not have their own e-mail system they could use at school. Karim went to work, and in a short while, an e-mail system for teachers was in place.

Karim's work during his high school years did not stop there. As a high school senior, Karim was hired to create a Web site for the research lab where his mother worked at the University of Minnesota. Unlike the high school e-mail system, the Web site work was a paying job. Karim was paid eight dollars an hour for his work. Not only was Karim working in an area he loved, he was getting paid for it, too.

In 1997 Karim graduated from St. Paul Central High School. Upon graduation, Karim had no doubt that he wanted to enroll

Karim attended the University of Illinois at Urbana-Champaign. One of the reasons he chose this university was because of alumnus Marc Andreessen, pictured, who had developed Netscape while attending the university.

in the University of Illinois at Urbana-Champaign, where he planned to study computer science. Karim sent in his application and awaited word on whether he would be accepted into the program. When Karim got his letter, it was not what he had expected. He had been accepted into the university, but not into the computer science program because that program was already full. Karim was disappointed, but he was not ready to give up. Karim wrote a letter back asking if the decision could be reconsidered. In his letter he wrote that he would be a "highly motivated, dedicated, and ambitious student"[20] at the school. Karim's persistence paid off. The school agreed to admit him into the computer science program.

One of the reasons Karim chose this particular university was because he admired one of the school's **alumni**—Marc Andreessen. Andreessen and others had developed the popular Netscape **Web browser** while attending the university. Karim says, "It wasn't like I wanted to be the next Marc Andreessen, but I thought it would be cool to be in the same place."[21] While attending the University of Illinois at Urbana-Champaign, Karim won many awards and scholarships.

In 2000 Karim left school early, in his junior year, to take a job as a technical architect with the PayPal company. Even when he left, however, Karim knew that at some point he wanted to finish his degree. By taking online classes and later attending Santa Clara University in California, Karim was able to earn his bachelor's degree in computer science and engineering in 2004.

YouTube

While at PayPal, Karim became acquainted with coworkers Steve Chen and Chad Hurley. This friendship eventually led to the

YouTube venture. According to most sources, Karim did not attend the dinner party where the idea for YouTube first originated, but all the men agree that Karim played an important role in YouTube's development. At times, Karim has been overlooked as one of the YouTube founders. Chen and Hurley seem to get most of the publicity, but Karim says there is no doubt that in order to get the site up and running, "it took the three of us."[22]

A Change of Plans

Early on in the YouTube development, Karim made a decision. He wanted to go back to school. He, Chen, and Hurley decided that instead of staying on as an employee of the business, Karim would become an informal advisor. At that time, Karim headed to Stanford University to obtain his master's and doctoral degrees in computer studies. Karim calls himself a nerd who gets extremely excited about the learning process. After completing his advanced degrees, Karim hopes to be able to share his knowledge with others as a college professor.

Along with his schoolwork, Karim is at work on a new project. His latest endeavor is called YouNiversity Ventures. Karim and his new partners, Kevin Hartz and Keith Rabois, are now helping other young people succeed in their own business ventures. The YouNiversity team works with former and current Stanford University and University of Illinois at Urbana-Champaign students who have their own ideas for innovative products. The men at YouNiversity assist others in realizing their business dreams by sharing their knowledge, acting as mentors, and helping them secure financing for their projects.

Even though Karim did not take on a large role in the day-to-day operations at YouTube, he visits the site often. He calls

Early in the YouTube development phase, Karim decided that he wanted to go back to school and left the business to attend Stanford University, pictured.

himself a "YouTube power user [and] one of the biggest YouTube fans in the world."[23] Asked about his plans for the future, Karim says he wants to find interesting projects on which to work. He most admires innovators, whom he describes as people who try wacky things that end up turning out well. Certainly, when these three young men first started working on YouTube, many people probably thought the idea *was* wacky. But they never lost sight of their dreams—and just look at them now.

Steve Chen, Chad Hurley, and Jawed Karim were only in their twenties when the idea for YouTube came about. When they recognized their idea could be useful for people all around the world, they pooled their talents and set out to develop their product. Even though the odds were probably against this group of young men, they each relied on their particular strengths and put in long hours to make YouTube a success.

Notes

Introduction: A Video Sharing Phenomenon

1. Quoted in Darren Waters, "Video Service YouTube Grows Up," BBC News, June 20, 2007. http://news.bbc.co.uk/2/hi/technology/6221588.stm.
2. Quoted in Committee of 100 16th Annual Conference Interview, "Personal Journey with Steve Chen," YouTube, April 19–21, 2007. www.youtube.com/results?search_query=Personal+journey+with+Steve+Chen&search_type=.

Chapter One: The YouTube Story

3. Quoted in Evan Carmichael, "Lesson #1: Create a Better Experience," EvanCarmichael.com. www.evancarmichael.com/Famous-Entrepreneurs/1172/Lesson-1-Create-a-Better-User-Experience.html.
4. Quoted in Carmichael, "Lesson #1."
5. Quoted in Oprah.com, "YouTube's Greatest Hits with the Billionaire Founders," November 6, 2007. www.oprah.com/media/20080601_tows_0053001002ATSCHADANDSTEVE_O_VIDEO_1.
6. Quoted in Committee of 100 16th Annual Conference Interview, "Personal Journey with Steve Chen."
7. Quoted in Mike Urban, "Meet the Mega-Millionaire," *Reading (PA) Eagle*, October 25, 2006, pp. A1–A2.
8. Quoted in Laura Sydell, "NBC Plugs into YouTube's Viral

Growth," NPR, June 28, 2006. www.npr.org/templates/story/story.php?storyId=5516885.

9. Quoted in YouTube, "Press Release: YouTube Speaks Your Language," June 19, 2007. www.youtube.com/press_room_entry?entry=sbopYZ18uVQ.

Chapter Two: Steve Chen

10. Quoted in Committee of 100 16th Annual Conference Interview, "Personal Journey with Steve Chen."
11. John Cloud, "The YouTube Gurus," *Time*, December 25, 2006.
12. Quoted in Committee of 100 16th Annual Conference Interview, "Personal Journey with Steve Chen."
13. Quoted in Cloud, "The YouTube Gurus."

Chapter Three: Chad Hurley

14. Quoted in Urban, "Meet the Mega-Millionaire," pp. A1–A2.
15. Quoted in Urban, "Meet the Mega-Millionaire," pp. A1–A2.
16. Quoted in Cloud, "The YouTube Gurus."
17. Quoted in Urban, "Meet the Mega-Millionaire," pp. A1–A2.

Chapter Four: Jawed Karim

18. Quoted in John Reinan, "Whiz Kid: Jawed Karim, a Graduate of St. Paul Central," *Minneapolis Star Tribune*, February 8, 2007. www. startribune.com/business/11209191.html.
19. Quoted in Reinan, "Whiz Kid."
20. Jawed Karim, University of Illinois at Urbana-Champaign Commencement Address, May 13, 2007. www.cs.uiuc.edu/mm/videos/articles/Karim2007commencement.html.

21. Quoted in Miguel Helft, "YouTube Founder Has Class," *San Diego Union-Tribune*, October 12, 2006. www.signonsandiego.com/uniontrib/20061012/news_1b12youtube.html.
22. Quoted in Jim Hopkins, "Surprise! There's a Third YouTube Co-founder," *USA Today*, October 12, 2006, p. 2B.
23. Quoted in Reinan, "Whiz Kid."

Glossary

alumni: Graduates or former students of a particular school.

blogs: Short for Weblogs, these are online diaries or journals.

copyright infringement: Using material owned by others without their permission.

interactive: A program or Web site that allows its users to participate in some way.

jack-of-all-trades: A person who can do many different kinds of work.

logo: A design used by a company for advertising purposes.

pop culture: Something that is commonly liked or approved of by many people.

upload: To transfer data from one computer's memory into that of another.

ventures: Possibly risky business projects.

viral: In computer terms, something that spreads or gains popularity rapidly.

Web browser: Computer software that allows an Internet user to search for information.

For Further Exploration

Periodicals

John Cloud, "The YouTube Gurus," *Time*, December 25, 2006.

Mike Urban, "Meet the Mega-Millionaire," *Reading (PA) Eagle*, October 25, 2006.

Web Sites

The First Ever YouTube Video (www.youtube.com/watch?v=jNQXAC9IVRw). Check out this short video starring YouTube founder Jawed Karim—the very first YouTube video.

Google Buy Out Announcement (www.youtube.com/watch?v=QCVxQ_3Ejkg&feature=related). In this YouTube video clip, Steve Chen and Chad Hurley announce the sale of YouTube to Google.

Steve Chen Interview (www.youtube.com/results?search_query=committee+of+100+conference%2BChen&search_type=). Find out more about YouTube founder Steve Chen in this six-part Committee of 100 interview.

The YouTube Blog (www.youtube.com/blog). This Weblog keeps readers current on what is happening in the world of YouTube.

Index

Picture Credits

Cover photo: Alberto E. Rodriguez/Getty Images

AP Images, 7, 12, 15, 20, 22, 26, 29, 33

Bryan Bedder/Getty Images, 14

© Mario Guzman/epa/Corbis, 30

Jason Merritt/FilmMagic/Getty Images, 19

Nancy Nehring/Scoopt/Getty Images, 38

Samantha Sin/AFP/Getty Images, 11

Robert Sullivan/AFP/Getty Images, 23

Mario Tama/Getty Images, 35

About the Author

Katy S. Duffield has been writing for children and young adults for over ten years. Her other KidHaven Press books include *Mysterious Encounters: Poltergeists, Innovators: Ken Kutaragi: PlayStation,* and *Mysterious Encounters: Bermuda Triangle.* Katy also writes picture books for younger readers and has written for many children's magazines.